Bannockburn School Dist. 106
2165 Telegraph Road
Bannockburn, Illinois 60015

If Dogs Were Dinosaurs

BY David M. Schwartz

ILLUSTRATED BY James Warhola

Scholastic Press/New York

Dear Reader,

When I was young, I loved to think about the sizes of things. One of my favorite songs went something like this:

> *If ants were elephants and elephants were ants . . .*
> *I could squash an elephant!*

Imagine being able to squash an elephant! I didn't really want to do such a thing, but that song got me wondering. . . . What if my dog were the size of a dinosaur? I loved the idea of walking my *T. rex*-sized dog down the street! How much food would she eat every day? I couldn't wait to find out!

This is a book about sizes of things compared to each other. We call this relative size. You will see some of the hilarious results when big things become much smaller, and small things become much bigger. For example, if a submarine sandwich grew to be the size of a real submarine, all of its ingredients would grow proportionally to the sandwich. With a little bit of math, you can see how much bigger the sandwich would become—and then you could figure out what would happen to the meat, the cheese, and the sliced pickles!

I've always loved math, and I've had lots of fun using it to answer the zany questions I like to invent. I hope you'll have fun, too, and that *you'll* invent some questions of your own.

And now, my *T. rex*-sized dog is begging to go out. Uh-oh! See you inside the book! Happy reading—and happy math!

Your friend,

David

If your **dog**

were as big as a

dinosaur...

. . . his dinner would fill up your living room.

If **Ralphie** were as tall as a **redwood**...

... his big sister could land a hook shot on top of the Washington Monument.

If the **Moon** were a **marble**...

…you could play baseball with planet Earth.

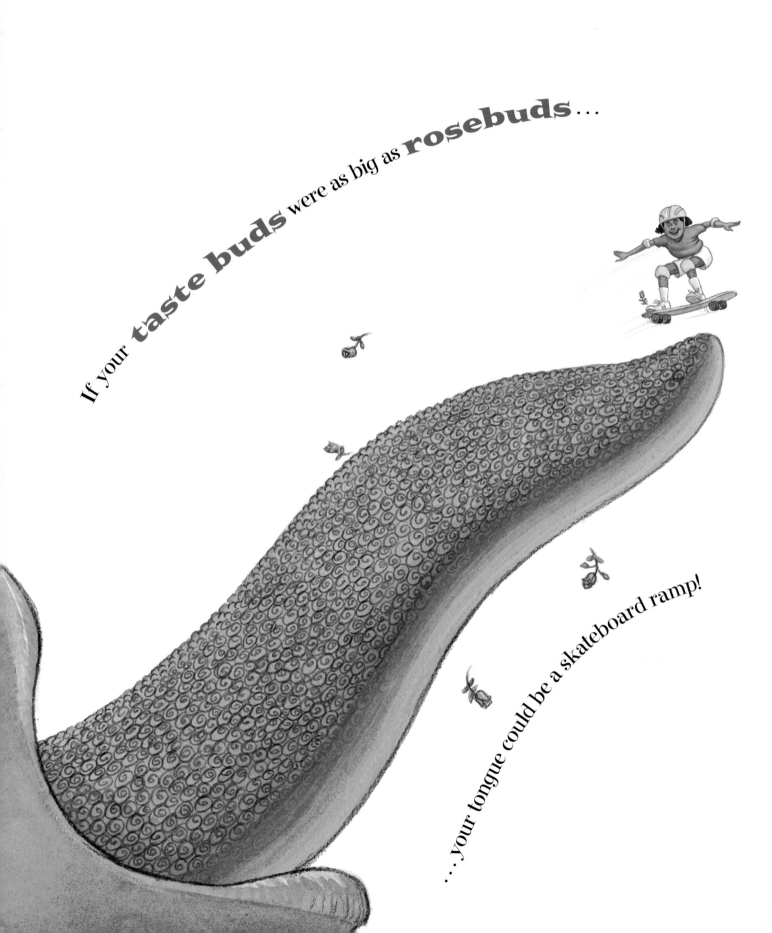

If your **taste buds** were as big as **rosebuds**…

…your tongue could be a skateboard ramp!

If **germs** were as big as **gerbils**…

... your handkerchief could cover a city the size of San Francisco—more than 80 times!!!

If **cruise ships** were the size of kayaks …

. . . speedboats could race across your cereal bowl.

If the **Milky Way** filled the **U.S.A.**...

...the solar system could fit in the palm of your hand.

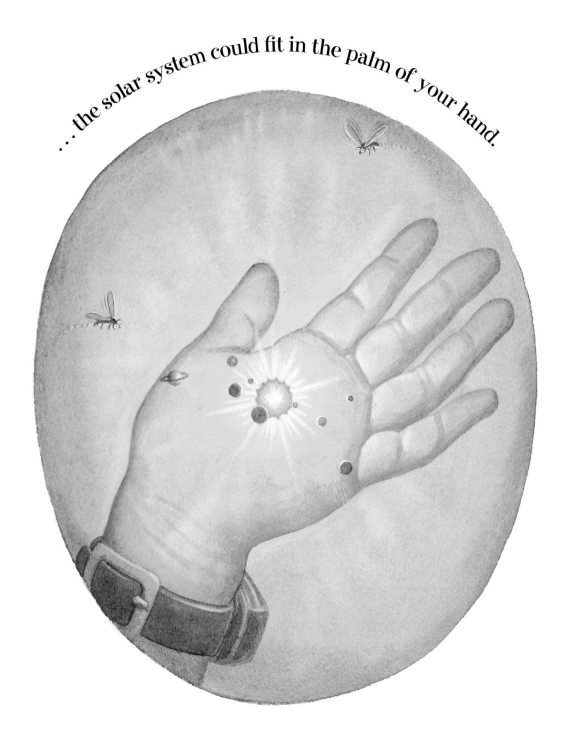

If you made **mountains** out of **molehills**...

... the mole would tower over the Empire State Building.

If a **submarine sandwich** were a **real submarine** . . .

... a pickle slice
could save your life!

If a **chocolate bar** covered the **mall**…

…each almond would be the size of a blimp.

If your **hair** were as thick as **spaghetti**...

. . . the meatballs would be as big as bowling balls.

IF YOUR DOG WERE AS BIG AS A DINOSAUR . . .

Imagine a dog, Rex, who weighs 40 pounds and eats one bowl of food each day. Now let's imagine that Rex suddenly becomes as big as a *T. rex* weighing 14,000 pounds. What would happen to Rex's dinner?

Let's assume that dogs eat according to their weight. If a 40-lb dog eats one bowl of food each day, an 80-lb dog would eat two bowls of the same size, and a 120-lb dog would eat three. A dog the size of a *T. rex*, weighing 14,000 lbs, is 350 times as heavy as a 40-lb dog (because 14,000 ÷ 40 = 350). So, a *T. rex*-sized dog would eat 350 bowls of food. They would probably cover every surface in your living room, and then some.

(In reality, a big dog that weighs twice as much as a smaller dog eats more, but not quite twice as much as the smaller dog. But the number of bowls of food that a *T. rex*-sized dog would eat would still be numerous enough to fill up a room.)

How much does a cat eat every day? How much more would your cat eat if it were as big as a *velociraptor*?

IF RALPHIE WERE AS TALL AS A REDWOOD . . .

Ralphie is 3 feet tall. A tall (but not the tallest) redwood tree might be 240 feet, or 80 times as high as Ralphie. His 5-ft-tall big sister is a basketball star. With her arm outstretched, she reaches up to 6' 4", or 6.33 feet. If she were to increase proportionally in size with Ralphie's growth, we would have to multiply her 6.33-ft reach by 80 to get about 500 feet. The Washington Monument is about 550 feet high, so she could do a hook shot to get the ball into a hoop on top of the monument. Of course, she could also do a layup, but she likes to show off her hook shot!

If you were as tall as a redwood, how many times as tall as your current height would you be? To find out, divide a redwood's height by your height. Now imagine other people growing by that much. Find out how tall they would be.

IF THE MOON WERE A MARBLE . . .

The diameter of the Moon at its equator is 3,476 kilometers. The diameter of the Earth is 12,756 kilometers. So the Earth's diameter is about 3.67 times as large as the Moon's. Imagine shrinking the Moon to the size of a 2-cm marble. Since the Earth is 3.67 times as large as the Moon, it would shrink to a sphere that is 3.67 x 2 centimeters in diameter, which is 7.34 centimeters. That's about the size of a baseball.

Look up the size of another planet, like Jupiter. How many times bigger is Jupiter than our Moon? How big would it be if the Moon were the size of a marble? What could you do with a ball that size?

IF TASTE BUDS WERE AS BIG AS ROSEBUDS . . .

Taste buds are tiny, onion-shaped organs found on little mounds, or papillae, that cover your tongue. Taste buds range from 30 to 70 microns in width. Let's pick a taste bud that's 50 microns, which is the same as .05 millimeters. Rosebuds vary in size, but a rosebud might well be 1.25 centimeters (or 12.5 millimeters) in diameter. So rosebuds are about 250 times as large as taste buds. Suppose your taste buds grew to be 250 times as large as they are now, so they would be the size of rosebuds. Of course, your mouth and everything inside of it (including your tongue) would also have to grow proportionally, or the taste buds wouldn't fit in your mouth! Your tongue is probably about 6 centimeters long (it goes further back in your mouth than what you see when you stick out your tongue). If it became 250 times as large, it would be 1,500 centimeters, or 15 meters long—a nice size for a skateboard ramp. Have fun—and don't forget to wear a helmet!

What is the largest flower bud you can find? If taste buds became that size, how large would they be? How large would your tongue be?

IF GERMS WERE AS BIG AS GERBILS . . .

Colds are caused by viruses, germs that are about 5 to 300 nanometers across. A nanometer is one-billionth of a meter. Let's look at a virus with a diameter of 200 nanometers, which a scientist would write as 2×10^{-7} meter. Now let's take a gerbil about 10 centimeters in length, or 10^{-1} meter. The gerbil is 500,000 times as large as the germ. If germs were as big as gerbils, they would have to grow to 500,000 times their original size in all dimensions. Luckily for you, your handkerchief is also growing to 500,000 times its original size in all dimensions! How large would it be? First, let's measure a normal-sized handkerchief. It might be 20 centimeters on a side. Multiply each side by 500,000 and that's 10,000,000 centimeters, or 100,000 meters, or 100 kilometers, which is about 62 miles. A handkerchief that long on each side would have an area of 3,844 square miles, big enough to cover a city the size of San Francisco about 82 times! (San Francisco has an area of 46.7 sq. mi.)

Imagine if your pet were 500,000 times the size it is now. How big would it be?

IF CRUISE SHIPS WERE KAYAKS . . .

The largest cruise ships are over 1,000 feet long; many are almost that big. Let's imagine a 1,000-ft cruise ship that shrinks to be a 14-ft kayak. It has reduced its length to about 1/70 of the original. Speedboats generally range from 16 to 33 feet in length. Let's take one that's 20 feet long and shrink it to 1/70 its original length. It will end up being about 3 ½ inches long and it could easily fit into your cereal bowl. Hope it doesn't have a bad collision with a banana slice!

Suppose the Mayflower became as big as a modern-day cruise ship. How many times bigger would it be? Imagine your car becoming that much bigger! How long would it be?

IF THE MILKY WAY FILLED THE U.S.A. . . .

Our galaxy, the Milky Way, is a spiral with a central bulge and outer arms. The distance across the entire galaxy is about 950,000,000,000,000,000 kilometers or, as a scientist would write it, 9.5×10^{17} kilometers.

Now let's shrink the Milky Way to the size of the U.S.A. The distance across the U.S.A. (from San Francisco to New York) is about 4,700 kilometers, which can be written in scientific notation as 4.7×10^3 km. Dividing the size of the Milky Way by the distance across the U.S.A., we find that our galaxy's length is $9.5 \times 10^{17} \div 4.7 \times 10^3 = 2.0 \times 10^{14}$ (200 trillion) times the distance across our contiguous 48 states.

So, if we also shrunk the solar system to one 200-trillionth of its actual size, how small would it be? If you measured the diameter of the solar system at a time when Pluto and Neptune were as far apart as possible (on opposite sides of the Sun), the diameter of the solar system would be about 12.2 billion kilometers. (For this problem, we're leaving out the enormous orbits of the comets, which are technically part of the solar system.)

Dividing the distance across the solar system (12.2 billion kilometers) by how much we are shrinking it (200 trillion times) tells us the size of our shrunken solar system. We get 6.1×10^{-5} km, and that is the same as 6.1 centimeters—which means our tiny solar system would fit in the palm of your hand!

Look up the sizes of the planets and our Sun. Suppose you represented the Earth with a circle one inch in diameter. What size would you have to make the other planets and the Sun? Draw them to see what they would look like compared to each other.

IF YOU MADE MOUNTAINS OUT OF MOLEHILLS . . .

Garden moles are 5 to 8 inches long. As they dig their underground burrows, they excavate soil that piles up in "molehills." The molehills are typically about 6 inches high—roughly the same size as the mole. So if a molehill really were turned into a mountain, as in the expression, "Don't make a mountain out of a molehill," the molehill would become mountain-sized. Even a modest-sized mountain—say 4,000 feet—would tower over the 1,250-ft Empire State Building. If the mole were to be enlarged proportionally to the molehill, it would also become the size of the mountain. It would lord over the Empire State, giving King Kong quite a fright!

Instead of a molehill becoming a 4,000-ft mountain, imagine a real hill becoming that high. Find out the height of a hill near your house. How many times bigger would it be if it were a mountain? How big would your house be if it became that much bigger?

IF A SUBMARINE SANDWICH WERE A REAL SUBMARINE . . .

Submarine sandwiches come in different lengths, but you're hungry today so you're going for a foot-long sub. Real submarines range in length from 200 to 550 feet. Let's take a small one that's 240 feet long. For the sub sandwich to become a sub, it will be enlarged 240 times.

When you ordered your sub, you said you wanted pickles. The pickles are sliced, and each slice has a diameter of about one inch. Enlarge it 240 times and that's 240 inches, or 20 feet. If you were on a boat and a catastrophe struck, you'd be very happy that there was a 20-ft-diameter life raft on board.

If your submarine sandwich became 200 times bigger, how big would its ingredients become? Measure the meat or cheese in a submarine sandwich, and find out how big the slices would be if sub sandwiches were submarines.

IF A CHOCOLATE BAR COVERED THE MALL . . .

We just ate a chocolate bar with almonds. It was 12.5 centimeters (.125 meter) long. The oval almonds measured roughly 2 centimeters (.02 meter) long x .9 centimeter (.009 meter) wide.

We bought the chocolate bar in a mall that is about 500 meters long. Let's figure out how many times longer the chocolate bar would have to be to cover the mall.

Divide the length of the mall by the length of the chocolate bar: 500 meters ÷ 0.125 meter = 4,000 times as long.

Now we have to also multiply the dimensions of the almonds by 4,000 to see how large they become. The giant almonds are .02 meter x 4,000 = 80 meters long. That's about 260 feet. The largest of the Goodyear blimps, *Spirit of Akron*, is 205 feet long. Our almond is a little larger than the *Spirit of Akron*.

Suppose a chocolate bar covered your school. How big would the almonds or raisins or other ingredients become?

IF YOUR HAIR WERE AS THICK AS SPAGHETTI . . .

Human hairs range widely in size. A thick strand of hair might be 170 microns (or 0.17 mm) wide. Mathematically, we would say it has a diameter of 0.17 mm. Cooked spaghetti has a diameter of roughly 2.5 mm. Dividing the spaghetti's diameter by the hair's diameter tells us that the spaghetti is about 15 times as wide as hair. So if we placed 15 thick strands of hair side by side, they would equal the diameter of a single strand of spaghetti.

Meatballs also come in different sizes, but we're making small meatballs for dinner tonight, and they are about 1.5 cm in diameter. If they were to enlarge proportionally with the hair, they would become 15 times larger in diameter, or about 22.5 cm. That's just slightly larger than the diameter of a bowling ball (21.8 cm).

Text copyright © 2005 by David M. Schwartz · Illustrations copyright © 2005 by James Warhola

Library of Congress Cataloging-in-Publication Data

Schwartz, David M. If dogs were dinosaurs / by David M. Schwartz; illustrated by James Warhola.—1st ed.   p.   cm.

Summary: "Explores the concepts of ratio and proportion by growing or shrinking various objects to the size of other objects and comparing them"—Provided by publisher.

ISBN 978-0-439-67612-0

1. Ratio and proportion—Juvenile literature. 2. Arithmetic—Juvenile literature. I. Warhola, James, ill. II. Title.

QA117.S338 2005   513.2'4—dc22   2004019958   10 9 8 7 6   10 11 12 13

Printed in Singapore 46   First edition, October 2005   The display type was set in Latino Samba.

The text type was set in 19-point Elroy. James Warhola's art was done in pencil and watercolor on Arches watercolor paper.

Special thanks to Matt Friedman, Editor, *DynaMath* magazine,

for his meticulous fact checking of this book.